THE STORY OF THE UNITED STATES

THE CIVIL WAR AND RECONSTRUCTION: 1850–1877

by Amy Van Zee

Content Consultant
Dr. Brett Barker
Associate Professor of History
University of Wisconsin–Marathon County

CORE LIBRARY

Published by ABDO Publishing Company, PO Box 398166, Minneapolis, MN 55439. Copyright © 2014 by Abdo Consulting Group, Inc. International copyrights reserved in all countries. No part of this book may be reproduced in any form without written permission from the publisher. The Core Library™ is a trademark and logo of ABDO Publishing Company.

Printed in the United States of America,
North Mankato, Minnesota
102013
012014
♻ THIS BOOK CONTAINS AT LEAST 10% RECYCLED MATERIALS.

Editor: Jenna Gleisner
Series Designer: Becky Daum

Library of Congress Control Number: 2013945672

Cataloging-in-Publication Data
Van Zee, Amy.
 The Civil War and Reconstruction: 1850-1877 / Amy Van Zee.
   p. cm. -- (The story of the United States)
Includes bibliographical references and index.
ISBN 978-1-62403-175-5
1. United States--History--Civil War, 1861-1865--Juvenile literature. 2. Reconstruction (U.S. history, 1865-1877)--Juvenile literature. 3. United States--Social life and customs--To 1877--Juvenile literature. I. Title.
973.8--dc23

                                        2013945672

Photo Credits: Bettmann/Corbis/AP Images, cover, 1; North Wind/North Wind Picture Archives, 4, 9, 24, 27, 45; New York Public Library Digital Collection, 7; Red Line Editorial, 10, 30; Abraham Byers, 12; Christophe Cagé, 14; Bettmann/Corbis, 17, 34, 39; Mathew Brady, 19; Library of Congress, 20, 22, 37; Corbis, 28

Cover: Confederate general Lewis Armistead leads his troops against the Union troops during the Battle of Gettysburg.

CONTENTS

CHAPTER ONE
A Broken Union 4

CHAPTER TWO
A Fight for Freedom 14

CHAPTER THREE
War Continues 24

CHAPTER FOUR
Reconstructing a Broken Country 34

Important Dates. .42

Stop and Think .44

Glossary. 46

Learn More. 47

Index 48

About the Author 48

A BROKEN UNION

In the dark, early morning of October 17, 1859, a group of 21 men snuck into the town of Harpers Ferry, Virginia. Their leader, John Brown, was an abolitionist—someone who wanted to end slavery. He wanted to start a slave revolt, and he had a plan to do it. Brown and his men captured the federal arsenal, where weapons were kept. They hoped to give the weapons to slaves. But the military soon arrived and

Sixteen men died during John Brown's raid of Harpers Ferry.

trapped the men, capturing Brown. He was hanged for his crimes on December 2, 1859.

Slavery in America

Brown's raid at Harpers Ferry was an example of the great tension slavery caused in the United States during the late 1850s. At the time, slavery had a long history in the United States. African slaves had first been brought to the colonies in the early 1600s. Slaves were the property of their owners. They were not paid for their labor and were forced to work long hours.

In 1641 Massachusetts became the first colony to make slavery legal. Slavery quickly spread to all 13 colonies. But eventually people began to feel differently about slavery. By the 1800s, it was a

Slavery in the South

In 1860 approximately 25 percent of Southern families owned slaves. But most Southerners who were not slave owners still supported slavery. Slaves were viewed and treated as property. They could be bought and sold whenever their masters wanted.

Slaves were auctioned off to plantation owners once they were brought to America.

regional issue. Northern states had freed their slaves. But slavery continued in the South. Farming was an important part of the South's economy. Southern plantation owners relied heavily on the free labor of the slaves who worked in their fields.

Roots of the Debate

The debate about slavery went hand in hand with another issue: states' rights and the power of the federal government. When the states joined together to fight Great Britain during the American Revolution (1775–1783), each state was very independent.

In 1787 the Constitution organized a central government. Each state could still make its own laws, but the federal government had power over the states. For example, the federal government could collect taxes from the states. Many conflicts arose as some people feared the new federal government might limit a state's right to allow slavery.

Short-Term Compromises

One of these conflicts brought about the Missouri Compromise in 1820. At the time, the Union had 11 slave states and 11 free states—an even balance. However, more territories were applying to enter the Union as states. Slavery was allowed in Missouri Territory, which applied to become a state in 1818. But adding Missouri as a slave state would throw off the balance of slave and free states. As a compromise, Missouri was added to the Union as a slave state, and Maine was added as a free state. Congress also agreed that no new slave states would be added

After the Fugitive Slave Act of 1850 was enforced, anyone who helped hide slaves was punished.

north of Missouri's southern border. The compromise worked until the 1840s.

The United States gained more land after the Mexican-American War in the late 1840s. Americans wondered if Congress could limit slavery in these new areas. Another compromise was needed. The Compromise of 1850 said people in a new territory would decide if they wanted slavery. It also included a harsh Fugitive Slave Act. This act allowed slave

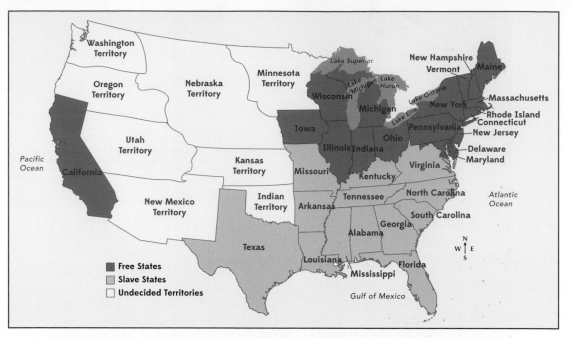

Slavery in 1856

This map shows the slave states, free states, and undecided territories in 1856. Compare what you see on this map with the information from the text. How does seeing this map help you understand why the issue of slavery was so important as new states were being formed?

catchers to go into free states to capture escaped slaves and bring them back to the South. With this act, the federal government protected the rights of slaveholders. And many Northerners did not like it.

A War Is Triggered

In 1854 the Kansas-Nebraska Act created the territories of Kansas and Nebraska. These areas were north of Missouri's southern border. They should have been free according to the Missouri Compromise of 1820. But the Kansas-Nebraska Act said that the people who lived there would decide if the areas would be slave or free.

The Kansas-Nebraska Act further split the North and South. Those who did not want slavery were angry that it might spread to new territories. They did not like that the federal government seemed to support the spread of slavery. The Republican Party formed in 1854 and only existed in the North.

Uncle Tom's Cabin and Dred Scott

Many events of the 1850s helped lead the nation to war. One of these was the antislavery novel *Uncle Tom's Cabin*. Harriet Beecher Stowe, a white northerner, wrote it in 1852. Stowe's novel depicted slave experiences in the South. Another event was the Supreme Court's decision in *Dred Scott v. Sandford* in 1857. The Supreme Court ruled that African Americans were not citizens of the United States. It also said that Congress had no right to limit slavery in the territories.

Abraham Lincoln was a Republican lawyer from Illinois when he was elected the sixteenth president of the United States.

Republicans disliked slavery and wanted to stop its spread into the western territories.

In 1860 Abraham Lincoln was elected president of the United States. Lincoln did not support the spread of slavery. The election seemed to be the tipping point for Southerners. On December 20, 1860, South Carolina seceded from the Union. People in South Carolina feared Lincoln would end slavery. They thought each state should decide if slavery would be legal or not. In the following months, Mississippi, Florida, Alabama, Georgia, Louisiana, and Texas also left the Union. These states now considered themselves separate from the rest of the nation. But the Union wanted to keep all states united. The United States was on the edge of war.

FURTHER EVIDENCE

Chapter One focuses on the tensions and events leading up to the American Civil War. What was the main point of this chapter? Visit the Web site below. Find a quote from the Web site that supports Chapter One's main point. Does the Web site offer a new point? Write a few sentences about the main causes of the Civil War and how slavery was involved.

Causes of the Civil War

www.mycorelibrary.com/civil-war-and-reconstruction

CHAPTER TWO

A FIGHT FOR FREEDOM

The states that left the Union joined together. In 1861 they formed the Confederate States of America. The founders of the Confederacy created their own constitution in February and ratified it on March 11. Jefferson Davis was named president of the Confederacy.

But the Union did not want to recognize the Confederacy. President Lincoln decided that federal

Confederates fire at Fort Sumter, occupied by the Union, on April 12, 1861, and spark the Civil War.

troops would stay at Fort Sumter in Charleston Harbor, South Carolina. This was an important port in a state that was no longer part of the Union. The Union's refusal to leave Fort Sumter angered the Confederates. On April 12, 1861, soldiers from South Carolina fired at Fort Sumter. The Confederates wanted the fort surrendered. On April 13, 1861, the federal troops gave up the fort. Nobody was killed, but the war had officially started.

The Confederacy versus the Union

After the war began at Fort Sumter, Virginia, Arkansas, North Carolina, and Tennessee joined the Confederacy. In May 1861, Richmond, Virginia, became the Confederate capital. On the other side, 22 states made up the Union. There were more men in the North. But even with this advantage, the Union had a difficult challenge. The North would have to invade the South and defeat its armies to try and restore the Union.

Nearly 500 Union soldiers were killed in the First Battle of Bull Run.

Soldiers and Leaders

After the shots at Fort Sumter in April, both sides built their armies. But the troops were not yet fully trained soldiers. Even so, Northern newspapers pushed for action against the Southern rebels. In July 1861, the troops fought the First Battle of Bull Run near Manassas, Virginia. The battle ended when Union forces retreated back to Washington. It was a discouraging loss for the Union. In November, Lincoln put George McClellan in charge of the Union troops.

Richmond and a Rematch

The war continued with victories on each side. In early 1862, Lincoln urged McClellan toward Richmond, Virginia. But McClellan was slow to move toward the Confederate capital. In June and July, Union and Confederate forces met in several battles near Richmond. McClellan faced a new opponent: General Robert E. Lee of Virginia. Lee and his troops forced McClellan's army to retreat. After the fighting, McClellan's troops left the area.

The summer would bring one last win for the

A Job for the Navy

Early in the war, Lincoln commanded that Southern ports be blockaded so the South could not trade with other countries. This was a big job for the Northern navy. There were more than 3,500 miles (5,630 km) of coastline to patrol and block. The Union scrambled to find enough ships for the blockade. Overall the blockade was successful in preventing supplies from reaching the South.

McClellan was a good Union leader, but he did not fully support the Republican president.

General Lee was recognized as a great general.

Confederacy. In late August, troops clashed at the Second Battle of Bull Run in Virginia. Confederate general Thomas Jonathan "Stonewall" Jackson's troops played a big role in defeating Union troops. Similar to the first battle there, the fighting ended with a Union retreat. More than 14,000 men on the Union side were killed, wounded, or missing.

Battle of Antietam

After a disappointing summer, the Union needed some good news. It came with the Battle of Antietam at Sharpsburg, Maryland, in September. It was the first battle to take place so far north. On September 17, 1862, Lee's army of 45,000 men advanced against McClellan's army of almost 90,000 men. The day became the bloodiest day in US history. More than 3,600 soldiers died. The battle was a draw, but Lee's army returned to Virginia.

Lincoln's Plan

This small victory was what Lincoln had been waiting for.

A Soldier's Life

Life as a soldier was not easy. Soldiers faced tough living conditions, including bad food and long marches. Sickness spread through the camps, causing many deaths. Dead bodies covered the fields after each battle. During the Civil War, one in five soldiers died. Soldiers used rifle-muskets with Minié ball bullets, which had been invented in 1849. Minié bullets loaded quickly and allowed soldiers to shoot better from farther away.

President Lincoln visits Union troops after the Battle of Antietam.

On September 22, 1862, Lincoln released his Emancipation Proclamation. This document said that slaves in rebelling states would be free as of January 1, 1863. This document did not actually free the slaves because the slaves in rebel states were still under Confederate control. But the Emancipation Proclamation greatly helped the North. It allowed African Americans to serve in the Union army. Many African Americans escaped to the North to help the Union.

President Lincoln had been preparing the Emancipation Proclamation for months before he issued it in September 1862. It read in part:

> *That on the first day of January, in the year of our Lord one thousand eight hundred and sixty-three, all persons held as slaves within any State or designated part of a State, the people whereof shall then be in rebellion against the United States, shall be then, thenceforward, and forever free; and the Executive Government of the United States, including the military and naval authority thereof, will recognize and maintain the freedom of such persons, and will do no act or acts to repress such persons, or any of them, in any efforts they may make for their actual freedom.*

Source: Abraham Lincoln. "The Emancipation Proclamation." Featured Documents. US National Archives and Records Administration, n.d. Web. Accessed June 21, 2013.

Consider Your Audience

Read the passage closely. How could you adapt the proclamation for a different audience, such as your parents or your friends? Write a blog post conveying this same information for your new audience. What is the best way to get your point across to this audience?

CHAPTER THREE

WAR CONTINUES

Fighting continued after Lincoln's proclamation. In April and May 1863, Lee's Southern army defeated Union forces at the Battle of Chancellorsville in northern Virginia. In Mississippi, Union general Ulysses S. Grant was attacking Confederate troops at Vicksburg, which finally surrendered in July. Vicksburg was an important win because it gave the Union

General Stonewall Jackson leads Confederate troops in the Battle of Chancellorsville.

African Americans in the Army

After Lincoln's Emancipation Proclamation, African Americans were allowed to join the Union troops. These soldiers faced danger if Confederates captured them. They could be put into slavery. Some were killed even after surrendering. By 1865 approximately 180,000 African-American men had served in the US Army. Many whites believed African Americans were inferior and treated them poorly. African-American soldiers received less pay than white soldiers until 1864. That year, Congress passed a bill giving African-American soldiers the same pay as white soldiers.

control of the Mississippi River and cut the Confederacy in two.

While Grant's men were fighting in Mississippi, Lee's army was pushing north to Pennsylvania. Fighting broke out on July 1 in Gettysburg, Pennsylvania. The Battle of Gettysburg lasted three days. More than 51,000 men were killed, wounded, or missing as a result of this battle. On July 4, Lee's forces retreated. Along with the fall of Vicksburg, Gettysburg was a terrible blow for the Confederacy.

Approximately 165,000 men fought in the Battle of Gettysburg.

War Life

The war was hurting all US citizens. When the war began, men volunteered on both sides. But as the war continued, the North and South used drafts, forcing men into war to bring enough soldiers to both sides. In the North, rioters protested the draft. In the South, there was a shortage of food, and prices began to skyrocket. Many on both sides were growing weary of the war, which did not seem close to an end. Some soldiers deserted.

A nurse tends to wounded Union soldiers.

Civil War Women

Women were also deeply affected by the war. Many lost husbands, sons, or fathers. Women were often left behind to take care of farms and households. This meant they had to manage slaves or work to make money. Many women in the North and South joined in the war effort. They baked, sewed uniforms, and wrote letters to the troops. Some even became army nurses. These women worked in army hospitals and on the front lines of battle to care for wounded soldiers.

Reelection

While the war continued, people gathered at Gettysburg Battlefield in November 1863. They met to remember the Battle of Gettysburg and to dedicate a new cemetery. At the event, Lincoln gave a short but important speech. He reminded his listeners that the United States was founded on equality. Lincoln honored the dead soldiers with his words. He urged the Union to continue the fight for freedom.

Andersonville Prison

Throughout the war, 194,000 Union soldiers and 215,000 Confederate soldiers were captured. Many captured Union solders went to Andersonville Prison in Georgia. It was built to hold 10,000 men, but it eventually held more than 30,000. Soldiers endured terrible conditions at the camp. There was little food, water, or shelter. Many men were wounded or sick. In 14 months, almost 13,000 prisoners died at the camp. Today Andersonville is a memorial site for prisoners of war.

Taking Sides

This map shows the states of the Confederacy, the states of the Union, and the locations of some of the key battles of the Civil War. Remember that to win the war, the North had to conquer the South. How does seeing this map help you understand the nature of the war? Where were most of the battles fought? What impact do you think that had on both the South and the North?

The next year, the Union faced more problems. In 1864 Grant faced off against Lee while trying to take Richmond and then Petersburg, Virginia.

Grant lost many men in the process. The year was also an election year. Lincoln ran against former Union commander George McClellan for the presidency. The presidential race was difficult. Lincoln feared he would lose, but good news arrived from William Tecumseh Sherman in September. Sherman's Union troops had taken Atlanta, Georgia, a major city. Northerners responded well and turned the election in Lincoln's favor. Lincoln was also strongly supported by Union soldiers. He won the election on November 8, 1864.

A Slow End

After Lincoln was reelected, Southern hopes for winning the war were low. Many men left the Confederate Army. In late 1864, Sherman and 62,000 of his men marched from Atlanta to Savannah, Georgia. On their way, they burned and destroyed property. They wanted to discourage the South. And they did. Many in the South realized they were losing the war. The end was near.

In January 1865, the Confederacy grew desperate. The Union had set up blockades. These blockades prevented Southern armies from getting supplies they needed. That month, Lee suggested that slaves be used to fight for the Confederacy. Confederate President Davis approved, but it was too late. On March 4, 1865, Lincoln gave his second inaugural speech. He spoke of the war's end and a desire for peace.

After a Union victory, Richmond was evacuated on April 2. The fall of the Confederate capital was one of the final blows for the South. On April 9, Lee surrendered to Grant at the Appomattox Court House in Virginia. Peace was on its way, but not before an act of violence would shock the nation.

Clara Barton was a Civil War nurse. Later in her life, she helped establish the American Red Cross. The following is part of a poem she wrote in 1892 titled "The Women Who Went to the Field":

The women who went to the field, you say

. . .

What did they go for? just to be in the way?

. . .

Show us the battle—the field—or the spot
Where the groans of the wounded rang out on the air,
That her ear caught it not, and her hand was not there

. . .

Did these women quail at the sight of a gun?
Will some soldier tell us of one he saw run?

. . .

Source: Clara Barton. "The Women Who Went to the Field." Civil War Trust. Civil War Trust, n.d. Web. Accessed June 19, 2013.

What's the Big Idea?

Barton begins her poem with a question. What does this question reveal about men's attitudes toward women at wartime? According to the poem, how did women help soldiers during the war?

CHAPTER FOUR

RECONSTRUCTING A BROKEN COUNTRY

After a busy day discussing plans for the nation, Lincoln went to see a play with his wife on April 14, 1865. During the play, John Wilkes Booth shot the president in the head. Lincoln died the next morning. The nation was stunned and saddened. With Lincoln's death, Vice President Andrew Johnson became president. And with the country facing reconstruction, there was much work for him to do.

John Wilkes Booth assassinated President Lincoln while he was watching a play at Ford's Theatre in Washington, DC.

Changing the Constitution

Steps toward reconstructing the nation had begun even before the war ended. In January 1865, Congress had passed the Thirteenth Amendment to the US Constitution. This amendment abolished slavery in the United States. But this raised many questions. What would become of the former slaves? What rights would they have, and how would these rights be protected?

On March 3, 1865, Congress voted to establish the Freedmen's Bureau. The Bureau assisted freed African Americans who needed food, education, jobs, and help starting their new lives. The Freedmen's Bureau helped set up more than 4,300 schools for African Americans.

Reconstruction Act of 1867

As well as addressing the abolishment of slavery, the United States also had to decide how to treat the states that had left the Union. President Johnson believed in states' rights and wanted to help the

President Johnson wanted to give the Southern states freedom to rebuild themselves.

Southern states. But others felt that the South should be punished for its rebellion.

At the time, Republicans led Congress. Many congressmen did not like Johnson's policies toward the Southern states. So Congress passed a bill, which included the Reconstruction Act of 1867. This bill divided the South into five districts. A military general commanded each one. These generals could remove state officials and appoint new ones.

Sharecropping

With the end of slavery, southern landowners needed workers for their land. Sharecropping became popular after the Civil War. Wealthy white landowners rented part of their land to workers. These workers were often former slaves or poor whites. The workers raised the crop and gave part of the earnings back to the landowner. Sharecropping allowed wealthy landowners to take advantage of others.

The Fourteenth and Fifteenth Amendments

After passing the Reconstruction Act, Congress focused again on the treatment of African Americans. Congress was aware of the challenges African Americans faced in the South. African Americans had difficulty finding good work with good pay. Some Southern states passed "black codes." These codes limited African Americans' rights. African Americans could not serve on juries or marry whites. Partly in response to this discrimination in the South, Congress drafted the Fourteenth Amendment. It stated that any person born in the United States was a citizen.

After the Civil War, freed slaves still faced prejudice and had trouble finding jobs.

It also said states could not make laws that took away citizens' rights. This amendment included African Americans. It became law on July 9, 1868. Congress made each Southern state ratify the Fourteenth Amendment before it could rejoin the Union.

In 1870 the Fifteenth Amendment was adopted. This law gave African-American men the right to vote. However, many Southern states found ways to stop them from voting, including poll taxes and literacy tests.

Challenges of Rebuilding

By 1870 all Confederate states had been readmitted to the Union. But the Southerners were facing big

The KKK

The Ku Klux Klan, or KKK, was founded in Tennessee shortly after the end of the Civil War. Members of the KKK disliked Republicans and their Reconstruction policies in the South. The KKK committed many acts of violence against African Americans and the whites who supported them. They wore sheets or robes to hide their faces while they burned schools and hurt free African Americans. They threatened, beat, or murdered people who might vote Republican. The KKK's violent actions caused some Northerners to push for stricter Reconstruction policies in the South.

changes. After the war, they had to rebuild damaged cities and farms. Southerners faced new laws and the abolishment of slavery. Many Southerners had difficulty accepting free African Americans. Some white southerners ignored laws that protected African Americans. African Americans faced much discrimination, especially from groups such as the Ku Klux Klan, a white group that terrorized African Americans and their supporters. Although they had their

EXPLORE ONLINE

Chapter Four shares a lot of information about what life was like for African Americans after the Civil War. The Web site below discusses how some African Americans were still forced into labor. What new information do you learn from the Web site? What information is the same? How do the two sources present the information differently?

Slavery by Another Name

www.mycorelibrary.com/civil-war-and-reconstruction

freedom, life was not easy for African Americans in the South.

As the 1870s continued, progress was made in preserving the Union. In 1877 the last federal troops were removed from the South. This was the official end of Reconstruction. But African Americans still faced racial prejudice and violence. The Civil War had freed the slaves, but African Americans' fight for equal treatment would continue.

IMPORTANT DATES

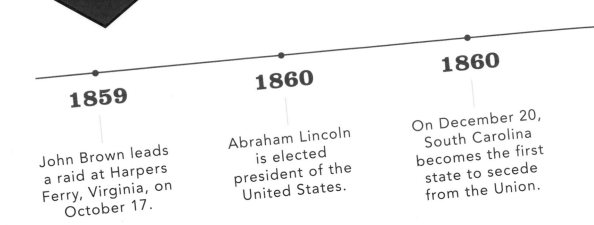

1859

John Brown leads a raid at Harpers Ferry, Virginia, on October 17.

1860

Abraham Lincoln is elected president of the United States.

1860

On December 20, South Carolina becomes the first state to secede from the Union.

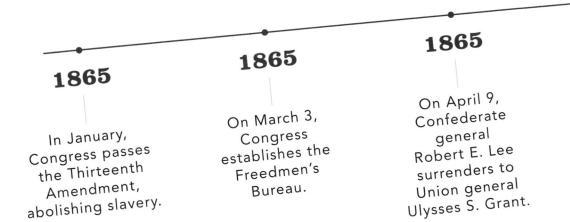

1865

In January, Congress passes the Thirteenth Amendment, abolishing slavery.

1865

On March 3, Congress establishes the Freedmen's Bureau.

1865

On April 9, Confederate general Robert E. Lee surrenders to Union general Ulysses S. Grant.

1861

On April 12, Confederate troops fire at Union troops at Fort Sumter.

1862

The Battle of Antietam on September 17 is the bloodiest day in US military history.

1862

On September 22, Lincoln announces his Emancipation Proclamation, which was to take effect on January 1, 1863.

1865

On April 14, John Wilkes Booth shoots Lincoln in the head. Lincoln dies the next day.

1867

The Reconstruction Act divides the South into five districts with military command.

1877

The last federal troops are removed from the South, officially ending Reconstruction.

STOP AND THINK

Say What?

Learning about the Civil War can mean learning a lot of new vocabulary. Clara Barton's poem in Chapter Three might have some words that are new to you. Read through the selection from the poem again. Look up the words you don't know in a dictionary. Then write each meaning in your own words, and use each word in a sentence.

You Are There

Chapter Two discusses what life was like for soldiers during the Civil War. Imagine you are a soldier fighting for the Union. You have relatives who are Confederate soldiers. Write a short journal entry explaining how you would feel after fighting in the Battle of Gettysburg.

Surprise Me

After reading this book, what two or three facts about the Civil War surprised you the most? Write a few sentences about each fact. Why did you find each fact surprising?

Take a Stand

Toward the end of the Civil War, the Confederacy considered using slaves to help them fight the war. Do you think slaves should have been forced to fight on the South's side? Write a short essay defending your position. Make sure to give reasons for your opinion and facts and details from the book to support your answer.

GLOSSARY

abolitionist
a person who believes that
slavery should be illegal

arsenal
a place where weapons are
made or kept

blockade
a war tactic in which one
side prevents supplies from
reaching the other side

desert
to leave the army without
being allowed to do so

emancipation
the act of freeing people
from slavery

literacy
the ability to read

plantation
a large estate that usually
grows crops and uses
laborers who live on the land

proclamation
a formal public
announcement

ratify
to approve

secede
to leave and no longer be
a part of an organization
or nation

LEARN MORE

Books

Gunderson, Cory. *The Dred Scott Decision*. Edina, MN: ABDO, 2004.

Pascal, Janet. *Who Was Abraham Lincoln?* New York: Grosset & Dunlap, 2008.

Stanchak, John. *Civil War*. New York: DK Publishing, 2011.

Web Links

To learn more about the Civil War, visit ABDO Publishing Company online at **www.abdopublishing.com**. Web sites about the Civil War are featured on our Book Links page. These links are routinely monitored and updated to provide the most current information available.

Visit **www.mycorelibrary.com** for free additional tools for teachers and students.

INDEX

Booth, John Wilkes, 35

Compromise of 1850, 9–10
Confederacy, 15–16, 18–20, 22, 25–26, 29, 31–32, 39

Davis, Jefferson, 15, 32

Emancipation Proclamation, 22, 23, 26

Fifteenth Amendment, 39
Fort Sumter, 16–17
Fourteenth Amendment, 38–39
Freedmen's Bureau, 36
Fugitive Slave Act, 9–10

Grant, Ulysses S., 25, 26, 30–31, 32

Harpers Ferry raid, 5–6

Johnson, Andrew, 35, 36–37

Kansas-Nebraska Act, 10–11
Ku Klux Klan (KKK), 40

Lee, Robert E., 18, 21, 25, 26, 30, 32
Lincoln, Abraham, 12–13, 15, 18, 21–22, 23, 25, 26, 29, 31, 32, 35

McClellan, George, 18, 21, 31

Missouri Compromise, 8–9, 11

Reconstruction Act of 1867, 36–37, 38

Sherman, William Tecumseh, 31
slavery, 5–13, 22, 23, 26, 28, 32, 36, 38, 40–41

Thirteenth Amendment, 36

Union, 8, 13, 15–18, 20–22, 25, 26, 29, 30–32, 36, 39, 41

women, 28–29, 33

ABOUT THE AUTHOR

Amy Van Zee is an editor and writer who lives with her family near Minneapolis, Minnesota. She has an English degree from the University of Minnesota and has contributed to dozens of educational books.